ISIS AND HATHOR

ISIS AND HATHOR

MOTHER GODDESSES OF ANCIENT EGYPT

JOY F. REICHARD, M.A.

Christina Tanner,
June, 2022.

party websites and their content.

Cover Art: Krystal Jenson

Visit the author website: http://joyreichard.com or http:celebratedivinefeminine.com

The publisher does not have any control over and does not assume any responsibility for author or third-party websites and their content.

ISIS AND HATHOR

MOTHER GODDESSES OF ANCIENT EGYPT

The Egyptian goddesses Isis and Hathor are often considered to be the same female deity. The worshipers of Isis borrowed, assimilated, and adapted Hathor's attributes to the extent it is often difficult to distinguish the two goddesses from one another. But while both embodied motherhood and family loyalty, the two deities are not the same. Hathor was more oriented toward femininity while the mythology of Isis is focused on transformation.

In this book, you will learn about Isis and Hathor, their similarities and differences, and hear several of their myths. Because Isis incorporated so much of Hathor, the focus will primarily be on Isis. Included is a guided visualization of Isis and a ritual with instructions on building an altar to her.

Who are Isis and Hathor?

Hathor, Egyptian Mother Goddess

Hathor is one of the most ancient of Egyptian goddesses. Her best known manifestation as the cow deity links her to Bat or Bata, an ancient pre-dynastic cow goddess that dates back to the 3rd millennium

BCE. The theory that matriarchal cultures existed prior to 3000 BCE in Old Europe, Anatolia, Egypt and Northern Africa suggests the possibility that Hathor may be linked to the original Mother Goddess and creatrix of the ancient Egyptians.

Hathor was the personification of the principles of love, joy and motherhood. As one of the most popular deities in ancient Egypt, she was honored by royalty and commoners alike. More daughters were named after Hathor than any other goddess. In other roles she welcomed the dead into the afterlife and was the goddess of music, dance, and fertility. She also aided women in childbirth.

Hathor is most frequently depicted with the snake, Uraeus, and with horns in which rests the sun disk. She frequently wears the *menat* necklace. This is a ritual necklace often inscribed with or bearing depictions of deities associated with Hathor, such as Sekhmet. The *menat* necklace was worn to provide good luck and fortune, and to protect against evil spirits. It was also worn for protection in the afterlife and is often found buried with the dead. When worn by women it possibly fostered fruitfulness and good health, while among men it possibly strengthened virility.

Originally, Hathor personified the Milky Way. In the third millennium BCE during the spring and fall equinoxes the Milky Way appeared to touch the earth where the sun rose and fell. Thus the four legs of the celestial cow Hathor, sometimes called Nut, were perceived as the four pillars that held up the heavens. The stars appeared on the belly of the cow. The Milky

Way constituted the heavenly water-way upon which the sun god's barge traveled, bringing day and night. In some legends, the Milky Way was seen as the Nile in the sky and was connected with the inundation of Egypt by the Nile. Hathor's birthday was celebrated on the day that the star Sirius first rose in the sky, heralding the coming inundation.

In Egypt, probably due to the fact that the goddesses and gods were worshipped for thousands of years, there is considerable assimilation and overlap of deity images and responsibilities. To the outside observer, Egyptian mythology can appear contradictory, confusing, and complex. To Egyptians, it seems to make perfect sense, and to even be complementary.

Hathor merges with many female Egyptian goddesses, especially with Isis. As Mistress of Heaven she is associated with goddesses Nut, Mut, and the Queen. As the Celestial Nurse she nurses the Pharaoh depicted as a cow or a sycamore tree. The fruit of the sycamore tree has a milky juice which was drunk as if it were the milk of the Goddess Hathor. "Take my breast that you may drink so you can live again," says Hathor to her son in one of the Pyramid texts.

As Mother of Mothers, Hathor was the goddess of women, fertility, children, and childbirth. She presided over everything to do with women, from conception or childbirth to health, beauty and matters of love and relationships. She was worshiped by both women and men. Her priests were both female and male.

Hathor was the goddess of beauty and cosmetic arts, yet she was not vain. She had an easy confidence about her own beauty and loved beautiful things. She was also the mistress of life. She was the embodiment of joy, love, romance, perfume, dance, music, alcohol, and was said to embody all the finer qualities of the female sex. Her fragrance was myrrh, and her stones were turquoise, malachite, gold and copper.

As the patroness of dancers, and because of her love for percussive music, especially the *sistrum*, her priests and priestesses at Danderah were also artisans, musicians, and dancers. She was also the goddess of sexuality. One myth tells of her rousing the sun god, Ra, from a deep depression by stripping naked in front of him dancing and displaying her vulva.

Myths of her husbands and children are complex and contradictory. In one she is the mother of Horus, the golden solar falcon who as the sun god flew from east to west. Horus was birthed by Hathor at sunrise and was swallowed at sunset as her consort in a daily re-enactment of the son-lover mythological theme. To the ancient Egyptians, each sunrise gave birth to a new sun, a new day, and Hathor was imagined as a cow continually giving birth and milk, thus sustaining the life which she has birthed.

As her consort, Horus was referred to as Horus the Elder by which she had a son, Ihy, god of music and dance. The three were worshipped at Denderah. Over the centuries her family relationships became increasingly confusing. First she was considered the wife of Horus the elder and daughter of Ra. Ra and Horus eventually were linked and became a composite deity Re-Harakty, and thus she became both the wife and daughter of Ra.

Then the relationships grew even more complicated. In some myths she becomes the wife of Thoth. Because Thoth already had a wife, Seshat, Hathor assumed many of Seshat's traits, which included reading, writing, architecture and arithmetic as well as acting as witness at the judgment of the dead.

Hathor also became the wife of Nehbkau, guardian of the entrance of the underworld. Another myth has Hathor as the consort of Sobek, another aspect of Amen-Ra, who had some association with Seth, the God of Chaos, who was the enemy of Horus and murderer of Osiris.

Hathor is also linked with Sekhmet. In one myth the populace was becoming disrespectful of the Gods and the Pharaoh. When Hathor found out she grew angry and took on the form of Sekhmet, the bloodthirsty warrior goddess, and set out to destroy the unfaithful. The slaughter was so great that Ra because concerned and decided to stop her. He poured huge quantities of beer colored a blood red on the ground to trick Sekhmet. It worked. Sekhmet drank so much beer believing it was blood that she grew sleepy and drunk.

She woke up hung over and lost her taste for blood. She then returned to her former more gentle manifestation as Hathor.

There is an intriguing association with Hathor, her temple in Denderah, and the Pleiades. In Egypt they are referred to as the Seven Hathors, who are associated with fate and fortune telling It was believed that the

Seven Hathors knew the length of every child's life, her priestesses could read the fortunes of newborns, and they could act as oracles of dreams. People traveled miles to seek out the goddess for protection, assistance, and inspiration. The Seven Hathors were worshiped in seven cities: Waset (Thebes), Iunu (On, Heliopolis), Aphroditopolis, Sinai, Momemphis, Herakleopolis, and Keset.

The Pleiades appear in ancient legends, manuscripts, and cuneiforms from around the world. They are included in the configuration of many ancient sacred sites. The earliest Greeks erected temples on hilltops that align with the rising or setting of the Pleiades. Several classical Greek temples, the Hecatompedon and the Parthenon, were oriented to specific positions of the Pleiades. In Mexico the ancient Aztec and Mayan worshipped the Pleiades at the culmination of the ritual lighting of the new ceremonial fire that took place every fifty-two years. Several Native American legends denote the Pleiades as a sacred place in the heavens. These are just a few of the references to the Pleiades in ancient legends and myths from around the world.

In Egypt the great pyramid, the Cheops, contains a fascinating mathematical correlation to the rotation of our solar system around the Pleiades, a total of 25,827.5 years. It is that precise! The Temple of Hathor in the ancient city of Denderah was dedicated to the goddess of love and the stars of Hathor, the Pleiades. The star clock in the temple celebrates the Pleiades, marking the greater center on which our solar system revolves, this same 25,827.5 years to complete the rotation. Half a world away correlations with this cyclical clock can be found in both Hopi and Mayan calendars.

Hathor is a complex and intriguing goddess who is surrounded by mystery and ancient lore. What can't be denied is that she was loved by the Egyptian people.

Isis, Egyptian Goddess

The cult of Isis borrowed, assimilated, and adapted Hathor's images and symbolism to Isis's own iconography. Because of this it is at times difficult to distinguish the two goddesses from one another. However, they are two distinct Egyptian Goddesses.

Isis, in ancient Egyptian mythology, is celebrated as the Great Mother. She is also the loyal and devoted wife who brings about the resurrection of her beloved brother/husband, Osiris. She is the patron of nature and magic, the friend of slaves, sinners, artisans, and the downtrodden. She hears the prayers of all, none are forgotten or overlooked.

Isis has gone by many names and played many roles in ancient history and mythology as goddess and creatrix. She was worshiped as one of the greatest goddesses in Egypt for over 3000 years, from before 3000 BCE until the second century AD. In the late 1st century AD many of her images passed directly on to the figure of Mary, Mother of Jesus. Her cult spread far beyond Egypt to most of the Greco-Roman world. It even spread as far as England, to the borders of the

Danube and the Rhine, and to the Arabian and Black Sea. To the Greeks she was known as Demeter, to the Romans as Ceres, and she played other goddess roles in many ancient civilizations. Pockets of her worship remained in Christian Europe as late as the 6th Century.

Her name, Isis, means *Queen of the Throne.* Her original headdress was an empty throne belonging to her murdered husband, Osiris. As the personification of the throne, she was an important source of the Pharaoh's power. Both Isis and her sister, Nephthys, were said to unite to protect the Pharaoh.

Isis and Nephthys were opposing complements. Isis was the light of the moon and Nephthys the dark moon. Isis was the dawn and Nephthys the twilight. Isis was the morning star and Nephthys the evening star. They were often depicted together, with their wings outstretched protectively.

The heavenly symbol of Isis was the star Sirius. This star was greatly beloved because its appearance marked not only the beginning of a new year, but also announced the advance of the inundation of the Nile. The inundation of the land by the rising Nile brought rich, fertile silt that replenished the soil which was vital for the survival of Egyptian civilization.

The Nile was central to Egyptian mythology. Every year the Nile died and was reborn along with Egypt. In mid-June, when the waters of the Nile shrunk to its lowest level, the lands were dry and dusty. The people and animals grew thirsty and hungry. Then in July the Nile began to swell again bringing water and the fertile silt. Life was once again renewed, and there was rejoicing and fertility. This theme of death and rebirth was central to Egyptian civilization and its mythology. This theme predominated in Egypt long before the advent of Christianity.

Story of Isis and Osiris

According to one myth about the origin of the Egyptian gods, Isis was one of four children of the sky goddess, Nut, and the earth god, Geb. The eldest was Osiris, and then came Seth. Isis was the third child, and her sister, Nephthys, was the youngest.

Osiris became the first King of Egypt and the creator of civilization. He is credited with teaching his people the art of cultivation and the honoring of the gods, as well as with establishing justice throughout both banks of the Nile. Osiris and Isis loved each other and became husband and wife. Their myth was to become one of the great love stories of antiquity. Nephthys became the wife of Seth.

Seth was obsessively jealous of Osiris and secretly wanted to dispose of him. One day Seth tricked Osiris to lie down in an ornate chest. Seth immediately nailed the chest shut and flung it into the Nile where it floated out to sea. Isis discovered what had happened to Osiris and was overcome with grief. She searched everywhere for the chest. Eventually, she learned that the chest had become part of a large tree that was felled and made into a pillar for the palace of the king of Byblos. In the myth Isis managed to retrieve the pillar. When it was taken down and the wood cut away, it revealed the sarcophagus of Osiris. Isis took it back to Egypt, where she opened the chest. She laid her face on the face of Osiris and kissed him weeping.

Miraculously she conceived and bore a son who was called Horus.

Isis then hid the corpse of Osiris in the marshes, while she left to care for her son. Seth discovered the coffin and, furious, tore the body of Osiris in to 14 pieces. He scattered them throughout the countryside, possibly throwing the phallus into the Nile. Isis, upon learning of this, once again set out to search for her husband. She found all but his genital member which had been swallowed by a fish.

Isis reassembled all the pieces and constructed a new phallus out of clay. She swathed all the parts tightly in linen bandages. Then the god Anubis performed the transforming magic of the embalming priest. Isis fanned the dead body again with her wings, and Osiris was revived to become the Ruler of Eternity. It is said that he now sits in the underworld in the Hall of Two Truths, where he has the power to judge the souls of the dead, which are weighed in balance against the feather of truth of the goddess Maat.

Several stories exist of the conception of Isis and Osiris' son, Horus. One implies that she conceived when she flew around the pillar as a swallow. Another implies that she conceived when she lay upon her husband in the boat. A third says that she took the form of a kite and conceived Horus while lovingly hovering over Osiris. Isis brought Osiris back to life with the beating of her great wings and the force of her love.

The legend continues with Horus, who has now grown up and sets out to avenge his father's death. A great battle takes place that lasts three days. During the battle Horus loses his left eye, which Thoth heals, and Seth loses a testicle. Finally Horus overcomes Seth and presents him in chains to Isis to put to death. Isis, however, releases Seth. Horus, enraged, cuts off her head. Thoth, however, replaces it with the head of a cow.

In a bit of political maneuvering, Seth then claims that Horus is an illegitimate heir, and that he, Seth, as the brother of Osiris, is the rightful heir (based on the ancient tradition of matrilineal descent). The council, however, rules that Horus is the legitimate ruler, thus instituting the patrilineal principle. Horus is crowned the new King. Seth, who represented the unregulated, chaotic powers of the universe, is now ordered to submit to Horus. Seth was thus mastered, and brought into right relation with the new order. He is also required to help maintain it.

Horus then journeyed to the underworld to tell Osiris of the events, to awaken him, and 'set his soul in motion.' Horus presents Osiris with his eye that was torn out in the struggle. This restored Osiris to eternal life. The eye became known as the Wedjat-Eye, the Eye of Eternity, which is said to protect people from harm.

As Osiris is revived, the spirit of life and growth are awakened, and the new year begins.

This drama of the death and rebirth of Osiris was re-enacted every year in the Mystery plays. The death of Osiris occurred with the drying up of the Nile, when life begins to withers and die. Isis is said to make the Nile swell each year with her tears of mourning for her lost love, her brother-husband. In this image the human and the natural world are united.

It was Isis' compassion and love, and her continual searching for and finding Osiris, that restored Osiris to life and brought back the return of the waters of the Nile. These events promised the renewal of life. Metaphorically, Isis became pregnant with the birth of Osiris in the manifestation of Horus, her son, which symbolizes the new year. **Osiris is yesterday – what has passed. Horus is today – the present which is full of life and potentiality.**

Seth was not so much evil as the inevitable opposing elements in the universe that have to be mastered. He is the antagonist. Where Osiris was moisture, Seth was aridity and dryness; where Osiris was the Nile, Seth was the desert that was ever threatening. Seth was nature – often unpredictable, threatening and destructive.

Isis knew that Seth, who symbolized the forces of nature as the Storm God and the God of Chaos, could not be destroyed. Rather a balance had to be maintained between opposites. This was the yin and the yang philosophy of Egypt. Right balance and right relationship was central to Egyptian philosophy.

Isis is the personification of the loving and compassionate power of the universe which resurrects life from death. She represents the act of loving kindness in the universe. Isis is the loving, devoted bride/wife, loyal and faithful. Because she loved Osiris, she searched for him and brought him back to life. But she was also, metaphorically, his mother. Isis, as the image of the devoted mother of Horus, represents the Great Mother, who protects, nurtures and cares for all of humanity

The spread of Isis' cult, and her appeal to such a wide range of cultures, was due to her humanness. The masses could relate to her. They could grieve with her for her lost love as the wife/bride, empathize with her struggles, and model her faithfulness. They could admire her courage, resourcefulness, and wisdom. They could feel protected and nurtured by her mothering qualities. She was the Great Mother. Many of her images were passed directly onto Mary, the mother of Jesus.

It can be duly noted that Isis borrowed, assimilated, and adapted Hathor to her own iconography; so much so that at times it is difficult to distinguish the two goddesses from one another. Both were the embodiment of motherhood and family loyalty. However the two deities are not the same goddess.

Hathor is the embodiment of joy, pleasure, beauty and of power and success that did not experience doubts. She basked in the realm of all that was feminine and had a close relationship to conception and birth. Hathor was single-minded in pursuit of her goals, especially in the form of Sekhmet, sometimes to the point of ruthlessness.

Isis is in many ways a much more complex deity. She suffered the death of her husband, her persevering loyalty enabled his resurrection, and she had to fight to protect her infant son. She understood the trials and tribulations of the common people. Isis could relate to them, and they to her. Isis was also merciful. Though Hathor welcomed the newly dead into the realms of the underworld, it was Isis who understood the death process and the struggle, pain and effort involved in transformation and resurrection.

Isis and Hathor have much in common, but they are not the same. They are two distinct and revered Mother Goddesses of ancient Egypt

ISIS
DISCUSSION QUESTIONS

- With whom do you most identify? Hathor or Isis?
- How are Isis and Mother Mary alike?
- How was Isis a composite mother, lover/beloved and Great Mother?
- Different from Mother Mary, Isis is also the beloved. What would the impact be on Christianity if Mother Mary was viewed as both mother and the beloved/lover?
- What do you think is the impact on our Western culture that the mother and lover/beloved have been split off from one another?
- We separate the good mother from the sensual lover in our culture. For those of you that have birthed children, did becoming a mother alter your sense of your sensual/sexual self?

- Why do you think Isis was honored and worshipped so widely and for such a long time in the ancient world?

- Why do you think right balance and right relationship was so central to Egyptian philosophy?

- How did Osiris and Seth play out the battle of balance and chaos on the cosmic plane? How did they manifest this battle on the physical plane?

SOURCES AND RECOMMENDED READINGS

Baring, Anne and Jules Cashford, The Myth of the Goddess, Evolution of an Image, Arkana Penguin Books, New York, New York, © 1993.

Internet Resources

Hathor, http://ancientegyptonline.co.uk/hathor.html

Hathor, http://egyptiandreams.co.uk/hathor.php

Hathor, http://Wikipedia.org/wiki/Hathor

Isis, http://isisoasis.org

Isis, http://en.wikipedia.org/wiki/Isis

Sacred Sites/The Pleiades,
http://shirleymaclaine.com/articles/sites/article-310

Additional Sources

Ellis, Normandi, *Feasts of Light, Celebrations for the Seasons of Life based on the Egyptian Goddess Mysteries,* Quest Books Theosophical Publishing House, Wheaton, IL, © 1999.

Regula, DeTraci, *The Mysteries of Isis, Her Worship and Magick*, Llewellyn Publications, St. Paul, MN, © 1995

ISIS
GUIDED VISUALIZATION

(This vision of Isis is based upon passages from the Wm. Arlington translations (1566) of a book written by the Roman writer, Apuleius, originally entitled Metamorphoses, later popularized as The Golden Ass. In this story he recounts a vision of Isis.)

Relax, and begin to gather all the pieces of yourself that have been scattered about with the busy-ness and the stress of the week. Bring them back to yourself and allow them to spiral right into your heart-space so that you become fully present right here, right now.

Begin to follow your breath, breathing in peace and calm, exhaling stress and tension… feel yourself sink deeper and deeper into a state of deep relaxation.

Imagine it is evening, with the Mediterranean Ocean spreading out before you. You can hear the sound of the waves, and you smell the salt in the air. The moon is full and the light of the moon dances on the surface of the ocean. Then from the shimmering moonlight Isis rises.

Brilliant from the sea, Isis rises… flower garlands crown Her abundant hair that falls upon Her perfect neck… Set upon Her forehead is a circlet of a mirror, attended by a serpent on each side… sheaves of wheat rise from the circle and shine like gold in the moonlight… Her cape is as dark as the night and gathers in folds beneath Her left arm… flowing over her right shoulder, all but covering the white linen undergarment that lays upon Her golden body…The linen is a fabric of the finest weave that is adorned with sprays of the crocus flower of the most brilliant yellow, the rose of red, and the flame of the brightest orange… Stars glitter along the edges of the blackness of Her cape; the stars circle a midmonth moon on this cape of midnight black… And upon the lowest hem that falls upon Her perfect ankles… the ripest fruits and the brightest of flowers weave an abundant border.

The fingers of Her right hand encircle the *sistrum* rattle that is adorned with the face of the mighty cow-headed Goddess Hathor… its thin copper discs of the rattle move along upon the narrow rods making bell like tones. Encircled by the fingers of Her left hand is the golden cup that forms a boat, its handle rising like a Uraeus cobra leading in the fore… Her palm branch sandaled feet are scented with the finest incense and spices of Arabia. …She is a magnificent vision.

- She smiles at you, and you feel a wave of compassion emanating from Her... Isis' presence radiates love... You are bathed in feelings of calm and inner peace and a wonderful sense of well-being... She has a message for you. Listen and receive it. .....pause 30 seconds.

- You may have a question that you would like to ask Her. Do so now... And listen for Her response...pause 30 to 45 seconds

- She has a gift or a symbol for you. Take it and place it somewhere on your body. ...pause 15 to 20 seconds

- Thank Isis for this time with her and for her counsel and wisdom...pause for 10 seconds

Now Isis begins to fade into the night sky. She slowly shape shifts into the moon shining brightly in the sky. The rays of moonlight create a shimmering dance upon the waters of the Mediterranean Ocean.

Now begin to gently come back to this time and this space. Feel your body in the chair... your feet upon the floor...feel the breath in your lungs....and when you are ready slowly open your eyes and stretch. You return to full consciousness remembering everything.

Adapted from Ancient Mirrors of Womanhood by Merlin Stone, Beacon Press, Boston, MA, © 1991, pg. 281-282.

RITUAL
CREATING AN ALTAR TO ISIS

You will be surprised at how your life may change if you create an altar in your home and take time every day to meditate before it.

You can choose any number of items upon which to build your altar. A dresser top, bookshelf, small table, or even a space on the floor with a pillow will suffice.

To create the altar first get a compass and locate the four directions (east, south, west, north) noting where each direction is for the room in which you want to place your altar.

On your altar place a symbol for air in the eastern corner (feather), a symbol for fire in the southern corner (candle), a symbol for water in the western corner (bowl or vase of water, or a sea shell) and a symbol for earth in the northern corner (stone or rock).

In the center place a statue of Isis or other deities with whom you wish to establish a relationship. Place candles to either side of the statues.

Placing a small bell to summon the attention of the Goddess is a nice touch. You can also add crystals, an incense burner, flowers, fruits or anything that you might feel called to place upon the altar. Sometimes the Goddess herself may inspire you by letting you know what she wants with an inner voice, or thought, or feeling, or sense of knowing that spontaneously emerges. I have learned to listen and honor these hits of inspiration.

Because of her relationship to magic, divination and intuition, Isis is believed to help develop intuitive and psychic powers. This is especially true for helping you cultivate greater trust in your own psychic wisdom. We have all talked about our "gut instinct" at some stage in our lives. Isis is believed to help strengthen this inner wisdom through her divine power. It is believed that she can also help clear the clutter in your head. When you meditate at her altar feel free to call upon her energy to help you think more clearly and see the "bigger picture". Isis is a goddess that offers abundance on many levels to those who worship her.

Isis can also enhance whatever divination tools you use, whether it be crystals, cards, runes, pendulums, or tea leaves. Invite Isis' presence to help you understand images or impressions presented to you during your meditations or your divinations.

ISIS TABLE OF CORRESPONDENCES

Meaning of Name	Queen of the Throne
Origin	Egypt
Family	Mother-Nut; father-Geb; siblings-Nephthys, Seth; brother/husband-Osiris; son-Horus
Areas of Influence	Motherhood, love relationships, death and rebirth, transformation, past live regression, intuition and perception. She is related to the third eye chakra, the center of illumination and insight.
Attributes	Loyalty, compassion, love, wisdom, intuition, resourcefulness, psychic powers, and inner strength.
Zodiac	Full moon
Elements	Water, earth, air

Trees	Sycamore, cedar, balsam
Herbs and Flowers	Tamarisk, flax, all flowers, lotus, all green plants
Foods	Grapes, wheat, barley, corn
Special Offerings	Wheat, corn, grapes, flowers
Symbols	Images of Madonna and child, rivers (Nile), scarabs, hair braids, cattails, papyrus, stars, (Sirius), ankh, throne, rattle, diadem headdress (circular disk with horns), cow, wings, milk, perfume bottles
Animals	Sparrow, hawk or kite, crocodile, scorpion, crab, snake (cobra), geese
Colors	Silver, gold, black, red, cobalt blue, green
Crystals & Gemstones	Ebony, ivory, obsidian, moonstone, lapis lazuli, dark aquamarine (indigo-colored stones)
Metals	Silver, gold,

HATHOR TABLE OF CORRESPONDENCES

Meaning of Name	Mansion of Horus
Origin	Egypt
Family	Mother-Neith; father-Khnum, Ra; Siblings-Ra, Apep, Thoth, Sobek, Serket; Consorts-Ra, Horus, Thoth. Nehbkau
Areas of Influence	Love, beauty, pleasure, music, dance motherhood, joy, fertility, childbirth, greet souls of dead in Duat
Attributes	Joy, love of feminine, lover of pleasure and life
Temples/ cities	Dendera, Deir el-Medina, Luxor, Island of Philae at Ashwan
Festivals,	November 2
Time of Day, Day of week	Dawn-gave birth to sun god, Ra, at dawn Wednesday

Zodiac	Milky Way, also both sun and moon
Elements	All
Foods	Beer, ale, grape, milk
Special Offerings	Beer, ale, grape, milk
Symbols	Sun disk set in cow horns with Uraeus, *sistrum*, ankh
Animals	Cow
Colors	Red, gold, cobalt blue, turquoise
Crystals & Gemstones	Turquoise, malachite
Metals	Gold, copper

ISIS AND HATHOR CIRCLE AGENDA

Intro: Name, city, a reason why they came tonight (10 min)

Casting the Circle: (5 min)

Talk – Who are Isis and Hathor? (30 min)

Discussion (15 min)

Guided Visualization: (15 min)

Ritual – Demonstrate how to create an altar to Isis – (15 min)

Group Share (18 min)

Goddess Cards (10 min)

Closing: Charge of the Goddess (5 min)

Releasing the directions – (3 min)

Total time 2 hours

ABOUT THE AUTHOR

Joy F. Reichard, M.A., is an Amazon Bestselling Author of *Celebrate the Divine Feminine: Reclaim Your Power with Ancient Goddess Wisdom*, the e-book *52 Weeks of the Divine Feminine*, as well as numerous e-books on various Divine Feminine Archetypes. With a Master's Degree in Women's Spirituality, Joy has led classes, workshops, and sacred women's circles since 2005.

Today Joy continues to use the mythology and legends of the Sacred Feminine as teaching stories helping women in their healing, transformation, and empowerment. Joy is the creator of "In Her Name Circles" which honors feminine wisdom and focuses on woman's spiritual and personal growth. In 2014 Joy launched "Persephone's Journey; A Wisdom School for Awakening Women." The schedule of her current classes can be found at **http://joyreichard.com/workshops/persephones-journey-school-for-awakening-women/**

Based in San Mateo, CA, Joy Reichard has a private practice as a transformational life coach, clinical hypnotherapist, and spiritual counselor helping visionary women and men who hear their soul's call to live their full potential and find greater joy and fulfillment.

More information on Joy Reichard can be found at **http://.healingwithjoy.net** and http://celebratedivinefeminine.com